Animals that Fly and Birds that Don't

David and Patricia Armentrout

Rourke
Publishing LLC
Vero Beach, Florida 32964

www.rourkepublishing.com

PHOTO CREDITS: © Steve Estvanik: title; @ Alan Liefting: page 4; © R Hughes: page 5; © Chris Fourie: page 6; © Iourii Tcheka: page 7; © Henk Bentlage: page 8; © Sebastion Burel: page 9; © Phil Morley: page 10, 11; © TAOLMOR: page 13 top/bottom; © Maungatautari Ecological Island Trust: page 15; © David Garry: page 16; © Christian Musat: page 17; © Armin Rose: page 18, 19; © Shannon Rankin: page 20; © Ulrike Hammerich: page 21 top; © Nick Baker/www.ecologyasia.com: page 21 bottom, 26; © Matt Edmonds: page 23 top; © Photolibrary/ Stanley Breeden: page 23 bottom; © Norman Lim: page 24, 25; © Lawrence Wee: page page 27; © javarman: page 28; © Grigory Kubatyan: page 29 top; © Photodisc: page 29 bottom;

Editor: Kelli Hicks

Cover Design: Tara Raymo

Page Design: Renee Brady

Library of Congress Cataloging-in-Publication Data

Armentrout, David, 1962-
  Animals that fly and birds that don't / David and Patricia Armentrout.
     p. cm. -- (Weird and wonderful animals)
  ISBN 978-1-60472-300-7 (hardcover)
  ISBN 978-1-60472-797-5 (softcover)
  1. Animal flight--Juvenile literature. 2. Ratites--Juvenile literature. I.
Armentrout, Patricia, 1960- II. Title.
  QP310.F5A76 2009
  591.5'7--dc22
                                            2008019692

Printed in the USA

IG/IG

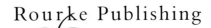

Rourke Publishing

www.rourkepublishing.com – rourke@rourkepublishing.com
Post Office Box 3328, Vero Beach, FL 32964

Table of Contents

Weird and Wonderful Animals

Whoever heard of a bird that can't fly? Believe it or not, quite a few **species** run or swim, but do not fly. Actually, scientists know of at least 40 species of flightless birds. Just as weird, a few animals do wonderful bird impressions. That is, they can fly or glide through the air to look like they are flying.

Wekas are flightless birds native to New Zealand.

Fruit bats are flying mammals. They roost
in trees and feed on fruit and nectar.

Large Flightless Birds

A male ostrich ruffles his feathers to attract the attention of a female.

Ostriches are the largest birds on the planet. They have big round bodies, long strong legs, and small heads atop long necks. Male ostriches get bigger than females; they grow up to nine feet (2.74 m), while females stand about six feet (1.83m) tall.

Ostriches have wings, but cannot fly because they lack long flight feathers. Ostriches put their wings to good use, though.

Ostriches eat plants and insects.

An ostrich's coloring helps it blend in with its surroundings.

Ostriches tolerate hot days and cold nights in the African **savanna**. They use their wings to adjust their body temperature. When the air is cool, ostriches cover their bare legs with their wings to retain heat. It is easy for them. They have wingspans of six feet (1.83m) or more!

Ostriches also use their wings to hide from cheetahs and lions. At night, they lie down and spread their wings as flat as possible over their bodies. In the dark, they look like mounds of dirt. If **predators** threaten, ostriches use their backup plan. They run fast and kick hard with their powerful legs.

Adult male
ostriches care for
their offspring.

Australia is home to flightless birds too. Emus are the tallest ones there. They grow to about six feet (1.83m) tall. They have small wings, long necks and legs, and three toes on each foot. Most birds have four toes. Emus have brown, shaggy feathers that keep them cool in the hot, dry climate.

Emu chicks lose their striped feathers as they age.

Emu eggs are dark green and weigh one to two pounds (.45-.90kg).

Did you know male emus **incubate** the eggs? Males sit on a **clutch** of eggs for about eight weeks, moving only to turn them. They don't eat or drink while tending the nest, so they lose about a third of their body weight during incubation. After the eggs hatch, males care for the chicks for more than a year.

The Cassowary

Cassowaries live in the tropical forests of Australia and New Guinea. They have black **plumage** and striking blue and red necks. These **prehistoric** looking birds have a tough plate, called a casque, on their head. They eat fruit that falls from trees, and use the casque to move debris when they **forage**. The casque also protects their heads as they move through the thick forest.

Cassowaries are aggressive and can be dangerous. They have long, pointed claws on their middle toes. When threatened by animals or humans, they cannot fly away. Instead, they fight with their long legs and big feet, and use their claws to slash open attackers.

Female cassowaries have brighter coloring than males.

Cassowaries can live 50 years or more.

13

Kiwi Birds

Kiwis are small flightless birds that live in New Zealand. So far, scientists have identified five different species. People rarely see them because they are **nocturnal**. Their **habitat** varies. They live in grasslands, pine forests, mountain areas, and along the coasts.

Kiwis are an **endangered** species. Young kiwis often fall **prey** to dogs, cats, and weasels. Adult kiwis are also threatened, but they can defend themselves with their speed, strong legs, and clawed feet.

Kiwis are the only birds with nostrils at the end of their long bill. They use their good sense of smell to locate worms and insects underground.

Kiwis are about the size of chickens, but lay eggs that are six times the size of chicken eggs!

Penguins

Most experts agree there are 17 kinds of penguins. One species makes its home on the Galapagos Islands near the equator. All others live in the Southern Hemisphere including Africa, South America, and Australia, but not necessarily on ice. Only a few species live in the Antarctic.

African penguins have black spots on their chest and pink glands above their eyes.

Penguins are graceful swimmers.

Penguins are **aquatic** birds, spending most of their time in the ocean. They have torpedo-shaped bodies that enable them to cruise through water. Penguins are flightless birds and have flippers, not wings. Strong flippers help them swim after their favorite foods: fish, squid, and krill.

The Emperor penguin is the largest penguin species. Adults stand 45 inches (114.3 cm) tall on average and can weigh more than 80 pounds (36.29 kg). Emperors live on the Antarctic ice and in the frigid surrounding waters. They are the only penguin species that breeds during the harsh winter. Groups, or colonies, move inland to nest. There, the male incubates a single egg while his mate journeys to the sea to feed.

Emperor penguins return to the surface after foraging for fish and squid.

An Emperor penguin slides across slippery ice on its belly.

Flying Fish

Fish and swim naturally go together. However, some fish do a good imitation of flight. Many fish have pectoral fins that help them swim and change direction in the water. Flying fish have long pectoral fins that help them escape predators. As they swim, flying fish pick up speed, and then propel themselves into the air. They open their pectoral fins and glide on the air currents created by waves. How far can they glide? Airborne distances are typically short, but some people have seen them gliding 100 yards (91.44 m) or more!

Flying fish gain extra airtime by pushing off the water's surface with their tail.

Flying fish inhabit warm tropical and sub-tropical waters.

Flying Squirrels

There are more than 40 species of flying squirrels; two of them live in North America. Flying squirrels do not actually fly because they're wingless. Instead, they jump and glide from tree to tree. These small rodents have a loose fold of skin on their sides connecting their wrists to their ankles. When they jump, they extend their legs and the skin opens like a parachute. They steer with their wrists and land by grasping a tree trunk with their small, clawed feet. Gliding distance depends on the species and the height from which they jump. A single glide can range from 5 to 150 feet (1.52m to 45.72 meters).

A pet flying squirrel gnaws on a nut.

Very few people have
witnessed the flight of a
flying squirrel. They stay in
their nests during the day
and glide around their
lofty habitat at night.

Flying Lemurs

Flying lemurs (sometimes called colugos) are gliders. In fact, they glide better than any other gliding mammal.

A mother and baby flying lemur cling securely to a tree.

A flying lemur can glide more than 200 feet (61 meters).

Flying lemurs have a thin skin that stretches from their neck to their front claws, and along their sides to their tails. They are clumsy climbers, but graceful gliders. They live in the trees of Southeast Asia. They sleep during the day and forage at night for fruit and tender leaves. To get from tree to tree, they jump, spread their legs, and catch air in their stretchy skin. They grasp tree trunks with their feet as they land.

Flying Snakes and Lizards

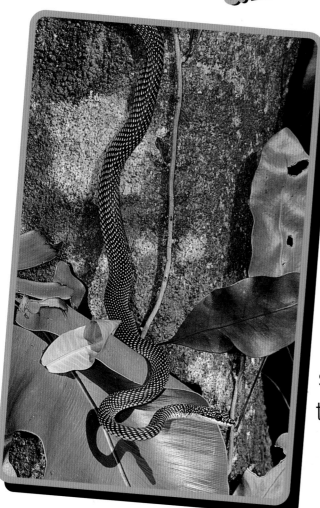

It is easy to imagine snakes living in a swamp or sandy desert. It is more surprising to learn that some snakes make their home in trees. Many snakes live in the rainforest of India and Southeast Asia. Five species are called flying snakes, but the truth is that they only glide.

Flying snakes eat other tree dwelling creatures like frogs, lizards, and birds.

Gliding lizards have wing-like flaps of skin. When they jump, they open their wings to slow their landing.

Flying snakes launch themselves from tree to tree. After taking off from a limb, they flatten their bodies and make slithering movements in the air to propel themselves forward. Since they lack wings, flying snakes cannot gain height; they only glide downward.

The paradise tree snake is one of five species of flying snakes.

Bats

Out of roughly 5,000 mammal species on our planet, bats are the only ones that can truly fly! Bats have wings with skinny finger-like bones covered with a thin skin. Bats are nocturnal and feed at night. Some species prey on small birds, mammals, lizards, and fish. Others eat fruit, and a few species live on the blood of other animals.

Fruit bats, sometimes called flying foxes, are the largest bats in the world.

A colony of bats can number from one to more than a million.

Most bat species feed on insects. They use **echolocation** to find them. These bats send out high-pitched sounds as they fly. They measure the time it takes sound to bounce off an insect and return to them. That's how they figure out where insects are in the dark! Their echolocation works so well that some bats can eat 600 or more mosquitoes in one hour!

Some bat species have large ears, which aid in echolocation.

Nature is full of weird and wonderful surprises. Animals that fly and birds that don't are just two examples. It may seem like nature played a trick on these unusual animals, but somehow they still found ways to survive.

Glossary

aquatic (uh-KWAT-ik): having to do with water

clutch (KLUTCH): eggs laid by a single bird at one time

echolocation (EK-oh-loh-KAY-shuhn): using sound and echoes to locate objects

endangered (en-DAYN-jurd): in danger of dying out forever

forage (FOR-ij): to search for food

habitat (HAB-uh-tat): the place where animals live

incubate (ING-kyuh-bayte): keeping eggs warm before they hatch

nocturnal (nok-TUR-nuhl): active at night

plumage (PLOO-mij): a bird's feathers

predators (PRED-uh-turz): animals that hunt others for food

prehistoric (pree-hi-STOR-ik): a very long time ago, before written history

prey (PRAY): an animal hunted by another for food

savanna (suh-VAN-uh): flat grassland with few trees

species (SPEE-sees): one certain kind of animal

Index

Further Reading

Ling, Mary. Penguin: *See How They Grow*. DK Publishing, 2007.

Lockwood, Sophie. *Bats*. The Child's World, 2008.

Mcghee, Karen. *Encyclopedia of Animals*. National Geographic Children's Books, 2006.

Websites

http://kids.nationalgeographic.com
http://pbskids.org/krattscreatures/login.shtml?
http://www.fws.gov/Endangered/bats/bats.htm

About the Authors

David and Patricia Armentrout specialize in nonfiction childrens books. They enjoy exploring different topics and have written about many subjects, including sports, animals, history, and people. David and Patricia love to spend their free time outdoors with their two boys and dog Max.